Recipes are tested, and instructions are provided for a TM31, but all
recipes can be easily converted for a TM5.

WHITE BREADS
White Loaf
Baguette
Pane di Casa
Japanese Hokkaido Milk bread
Four-ingredient Cheat Sourdough
Kaiser Rolls
English Muffin Toasting bread

WHOLE WHEAT, MULTI-GRAIN, and RYE
Country Style Rye and Caraway
Soy & Linseed
Whole Wheat bread
Brown Rice bread
German Vollkornbrot
Wholemeal Chia bread

GLUTEN FREE BREADS
GF Chia and Mixed Seed bread
GF Cheese and Onion bread
GF Honey, almond and cinnamon squares

SWEET BREADS
Yeasted Cinnamon bread
Raspberry Brioche
Choc Walnut Baba
Bun-ana Easter Loaf

WHITE

WHITE LOAF

The addition of the sparkling water makes this the softest white loaf ever, it will quite literally melt in your mouth!

Makes one loaf (approximately 10 slices)

Preparation time:
Preparation: 1h 30mins
Baking: 25mins

Accessories you'll need:
TM31/TM5
Spatula

Ingredients:
2 teaspoons dried yeast
1 teaspoon sugar
500 grams bakers flour
2 teaspoons bread improver (optional, but makes a big difference)
270 grams sparkling water (e.g mineral water NOT soda water), room temperature
1 tablespoon salt
15 grams olive oil

Method:
1. Add ingredients to the bowl in the order listed.
2. Blend briefly sp 7 / 15-20 secs until roughly combined.
3. Knead for 5 minutes.
4. Transfer to a Thermomat or greased covered bowl and rest for 20 minutes.
5. Punch down dough and roll into a 25cm x 25cm log, to fit your greased loaf pan.

6. Slash surface (if desired) and spray lightly with water. Cover and leave to rise 30-45 minutes, or until it has crowned 2.5cm above the edge of the tin.

7. Place into a cold oven set to 190C and bake for 25 minutes or until golden and cooked.

8. Cool immediately on a wire rack.

BAGUETTE

From the deliciously crunchy crust to the soft delicate inside, these baguettes are best eaten on the day!

Makes two (20-30cm long) baguettes

Preparation time:
Preparation: 1h 15mins
Baking: 25mins

Accessories you'll need:
TM31/TM5
Spatula

Ingredients:
300 grams water
pinch sugar
2 teaspoons dried yeast
500 grams bakers flour
2 teaspoons bread improver
1 teaspoon salt
25 grams oil

Method:
1.   Add water, yeast and sugar to bowl, and blend briefly to sp 4, to combine.
2.   Add remaining ingredients.
3.   Slowly move dial to speed 7 and blend for 15 seconds.
4.   Knead for 6 minutes.
5.   Tip onto a Thermomat or greased and covered bowl. Allow to rest for 15 minutes.
6.   Punch dough down and cut into 2 pieces.

7.   Roll each piece into a log shape approximately 20-30cm long.

8.   Place into your prepared baguette tray, or onto a paper lined tray.

9.   Spray lightly with water, slash tops (optional) and cover lightly with greased cling-wrap or tea towel.

10.   Leave to prove another 30 minutes or until doubled in size.

11.   Preheat oven to 200C.

12.   Spray tops again with water and a couple of times during baking to ensure a crisp crust.

13.   Bake for about 20-25 minutes or until cooked when tested. Cool on a wire rack.

PANE DI CASA

Bring the taste of Italy to your table with this delicious Italian house bread, Pane di Casa. Enjoy fresh or toasted and especially tasty slathered with your favourite topping!

Makes one loaf (approximately 12 slices)

Preparation time:
Preparation: 35mins
Baking: 30mins

Accessories you'll need:
TM31/TM5
Spatula

Ingredients:
2 level teaspoons dried yeast
1 teaspoon sugar
300 grams warm water
400 grams bakers flour
100 grams semolina
1 teaspoon Gluten flour
1 teaspoon bread improver
20 grams olive oil
1 teaspoon salt

Method:
1.   Place water, yeast and sugar into the bowl.
2.   Whizz sp 3/ 10 seconds
3.   Add all remaining ingredients, making sure to add them in the order listed. Knead for 5 minutes.
4.   Transfer dough to a Thermomat or a greased covered bowl and rest

for 15 minutes.

5.   Knock down dough, shape into a ball and press into a greased springform tin, about 22cm.

6.   Using a sharp knife or razor, cut a cross into the top. Spray lightly with water and sprinkle with polenta, poppy or sesame seeds.

7.   Prove, lightly covered, in a warm place until dough reaches 2cm over the top of the tin. About 30 minutes.

8.   Place tin into a cold oven set to 190C, for about 30 minutes.

9.   Cool on a wire rack.

JAPANESE HOKKAIDO MILK BREAD

Oh my... these are truly delicious and best eaten on the day they're baked, but then again: how could you resist until they're all gone?!

Makes one loaf of 8 portions

Preparation time:
Preparation: 2h 20mins
Baking: 25mins

Accessories you'll need:
TM31/TM5
Spatula
Measuring Cup

Ingredients:
Tangzhong (starter)
45 grams water
40 grams milk
30 bakers flour

Dough
60 grams unsalted butter, chopped
3 teaspoons dried yeast
35 grams sugar
380 grams bakers flour
1 teaspoon bread improver
15 grams non-fat milk powder
1 egg
40 grams water
1 teaspoon salt
extra milk for glazing
sesame seeds, for sprinkling

To make the tangzhong / starter:

1.   Add all starter ingredients to the bowl and combine at 50C / 3 mins / sp2.

2.   Leave in bowl and continue with the recipe. Or transfer to a small bowl and leave in the fridge for up to 3 days. Heat to 50C/sp 3 if it's been in the fridge, before continuing.

To make the dough:

1.   Add butter to the starter in the bowl and blend sp 3 / 10 seconds.

2.   Add remaining ingredients in the order listed, except for the extra milk and sesame seeds.

3.   Blitz to combine sp 7 / 20 seconds. Scrape if necessary.

4.   Knead for 5 minutes.

5.   Tip onto a Thermomat or a greased covered bowl and leave to rest for 30 minutes. It may not double but it will be puffy.

6.   Punch down and shape into 8 balls.

7.   Grease a 20-23cm springform tin and place balls side by side and one in the middle.

8.   Spray lightly with water, cover and prove for 50-60 minutes, or until doubled in size. Preheat the oven to 180C.

9.   Gently brush the tops with milk.

10.   Bake for 25-30 minutes or until golden brown and cooked.

11.   Once removed from the oven, leave the rolls to cool in the pan for 10 minutes before placing on a wire rack to cool.

FOUR INGREDIENT SOURDOUGH

This is a delicious crusty style bread with a definite "sour" tang that is perfect fresh, toasted, or topped as bruschetta.

Makes one loaf

Preparation time:
Preparation: 2 hours
Baking: 30 mins

Accessories you'll need:
TM31/TM5
Spatula
Measuring Cup

Ingredients:
400 grams bakers flour
1/2 teaspoon yeast, dried
385 grams natural yogurt
1.5 teaspoons salt

Method:
1.   Add all ingredients (in the order listed) to the bowl.
2.   Slowly bring speed up to 7.
3.   If mixture is very dry not coming together, add another tablespoon of yogurt. The dough will be sticky but should hold together.
4.   Knead for 2 minutes.
5.   Tip into a greased covered bowl and leave to sit at room temperature for 12-18 hours.
6.   Once fermentation time has passed, dust your bench-top with flour, and gently tip contents of the bowl on top of it.
7.   Gently fold envelope style, turning 1/4 turns 4 times. Try not to

squash the air bubbles too much. Shape carefully into a ball.

8.   Gently place ball onto a piece of floured parchment, cover with a large bowl and prove until doubled in size (1-2 hours).

9.   About 45 minutes before ready for baking, place your cast iron or (high heat proof) lidded pot into an oven set to 220C. Pot needs to be smoking hot when ready..be careful!

10.   Carefully remove lidded pot from oven, gently drop the parchment paper with the dough in it into the hot pot. Cover with the lid.

11.   Bake for 30 minutes. Then remove lid to brown for another further 5 minutes.

12.   Cool on a wire rack.

Thermify Me Top Tips:
* To successfully make this bread you need a (high) heatproof type of lidded dish. I have a cast iron camping style (lidded) pot that I save for this type of loaf.

* It still takes time to make. Allow a couple of days.

* Do not leave to ferment for longer than 18 hours and not less than 12 hours.

KAISER ROLLS

Delightfully chewy rolls are beautiful as an open-style roll filled with your favourite toppings. Best eaten (or frozen) on the day they're baked.

Makes 8-10 rolls

Preparation time:
Preparation: 12-15 hours
Baking: 25mins

Accessories you'll need:
TM31/TM5
Spatula

Ingredients:
Poolish
220 grams bakers flour
220 grams water
pinch dried yeast

Dough
425 grams bakers flour
1 teaspoon dried yeast
2/3rd teaspoon diastatic/ brewers malt
All of the poolish
220 grams water
2 teaspoons salt
beaten egg (egg wash)
poppy or sesame seeds for sprinkling

To make the Poolish:
1.   Combine the ingredients in a bowl, stir well to combine and leave at room temperature to ferment for 12-15 hours, or until bubbly and risen.

Combining the poolish and dough:
1.   Add all the ingredients, in the order listed to the bowl.
2.   Mix briefly to combine, sp 7 / 15 seconds.
3.   Knead 5 minutes.
4.   Tip into a greased bowl and cover with cling-wrap. Leave to rest for 1 hour.
5.   Punch down and shape as desired.
6.   Prove a further 30-45 minutes.
7.   Gently brush with egg wash and sprinkle with seeds if desired.
8.   Place in a preheated oven for 20-25 minutes.
9.   Cool on a wire rack.

ENGLISH MUFFIN TOASTING BREAD

With a texture similar to English muffins, this bread is the ideal toasty treat! Slather on some butter, honey, jam, or marmalade and taste the indulgence!

Makes one loaf

Preparation time:
Preparation: 1h 30mins
Baking: 25mins

Accessories you'll need:
TM31/TM5
Spatula

Ingredients:
25 grams milk powder
350 grams water
30 grams oil, rice bran, macadamia
1 tablespoon dried yeast
20 grams sugar
450 grams bakers flour
1/4 teaspoon Bicarbonate Soda
1.5 teaspoons salt
1 tablespoon cornmeal (polenta), to sprinkle in the tin and over the top of the loaf.

Method:
1.   Measure the water, milk and oil into the bowl.
2.   Set to 60C/ 4mins / sp2.
3.   Measure in the remaining ingredients.
4.   Blend at sp 5 / 1 minute. The mixture will be quite soft.
5.   Grease a small loaf tin (mine measures 21cm x 23cm x 10.5cm)

and sprinkle with the polenta. This is the only proofing this loaf requires.

6.	Scoop mixture into the tin, cover and leave to rise (covered) until the mixture crowns about 5mm above the surface of the tin. This can take up to an hour or more.

7.	When the dough is nearly ready, preheat your oven to 190C.

8.	Sprinkle the top of your loaf with extra Polenta if desired.

9.	Bake for 25 minutes or until cooked when tested.

10.	Remove from pan immediately and cool on a wire rack.

Thermify Me Top Tips:

*	If you don't have milk powder, use 150g water and 100g milk.
*	Please note that there is only one rise in this recipe.

WHOLE WHEAT
MULTI-GRAIN
and RYE

COUNTRY STYLE RYE & CARAWAY

A hearty and filling bread filled with seedy goodness! The addition of yoghurt to the recipe gives the bread a slight tang similar to a sourdough.

Makes one loaf

Preparation time:
Preparation: 1h 30mins
Baking: 30mins

Accessories you'll need:
TM31/TM5
Spatula

Ingredients:
200 grams water
2 teaspoons dried yeast
1.5 teaspoons sugar
100 grams rye flour
65 grams natural yogurt
260 grams bakers flour
1 tablespoon Gluten flour
2 teaspoons bread improver
1 tablespoon caraway seeds
20 grams olive oil
2 teaspoons molasses
1 teaspoon salt
1/4 teaspoon citric acid (optional, for extra tang)

Method:
1.   Add water, sugar, yeast and rye flour to bowl.
2.   Blend to a smooth paste, 10 secs / sp3.
3.   Leave to rest, covered with a tea towel for 20 minutes.
4.   Add remaining ingredients in the order listed.
5.   Blitz briefly, sp 7 / 20 secs. The mixture will be sticky, but if it appears too wet add another 30g of baker's flour.
6.   Tip onto a Thermomat or a covered greased bowl, and let rest for 20 minutes.
7.   Punch down the dough and shape into a ball or loaf shape.
8.   Place onto a baking paper lined tray, cover and prove for 30 minutes or until double. Slash top and sprinkle with flour if desired.
9.   Place bread into a cold oven and set temperature to 190C.
10.   Bake for 30minutes or until cooked when tested.
11.   Cool on a wire rack.

SOY & LINSEED

A delicious option for healthy and tasty sandwiches!

Makes one loaf

Preparation time:

Preparation: 2h 30mins

Baking: 30mins

Accessories you'll need:

TM31/TM5

Spatula

Measuring Cup

Ingredients:

Barley

65 grams pearl barley

900 grams water

Dough

250 grams water

2 teaspoons yeast, dried, or 30g fresh

1 teaspoon sugar

150 grams wholemeal flour

300 grams bakers flour

2 tablespoons Gluten flour (optional, but produces a superior loaf)

20 grams Soy flour

2 teaspoons bread improver

1 teaspoon salt

2 tablespoons olive oil

1 tablespoon Linseeds

Pre-cooked barley (see over the page)

To make barley:
1.   Place barley into simmering basket and rinse lightly.
2.   Add water to bowl and place basket inside.
3.   Cook at Varoma 30 mins/sp4
4.   Drain and cool under running water.
5.   Set aside.

To make dough:
1.   Place water, yeast and sugar into bowl and blitz briefly sp3/5 secs to combine.
2.   Add all remaining ingredients, including the previously cooked barley, in the order listed.
3.   Blend slowly by moving the dial to speed 7, using the spatula if necessary to help combine the mixture. If the mixture appears dry and crumbly, add a little more water. If wet, add a little more flour.
4.   Knead for 6 minutes
5.   Tip mixture onto a silicon mat or into a greased bowl and cover lightly to rest for 15 minutes.
6.   Punch down dough, trying to eliminate any air pockets.
7.   Shape into a loaf tin, or a free form style. Slash the top if desired.
8.   Cover lightly and leave to rise until doubled in size (30+ minutes)
9.   Spray surface lightly with water. Optional: dust with barley flakes, or bran/oats
10.   Place into a cold oven set to 190C for 30-35 minutes or until cooked when tested.
11.   Tip out onto a wire rack to cool.

WHOLE WHEAT BREAD

A moist and delicious whole wheat bread perfect fresh or toasted!

Makes one loaf

Preparation time:

Preparation: 1h 30mins
Baking: 30mins

Accessories you'll need:

TM31/TM5
Spatula

Ingredients:

125 grams water
1/4 cup milk
3 teaspoons dried yeast
1 tablespoon honey
1 tablespoon molasses
300 grams bakers flour
250 grams wholemeal flour
2 teaspoons bread improver
1 tablespoon Gluten flour
2 tablespoons olive oil
1 teaspoon salt
2 teaspoons bran flakes for sprinkling, optional

Method:

1.   Add milk and water to bowl.
2.   Heat to 37C / 3min / sp soft speed.
3.   Add yeast, honey and molasses. Blend briefly sp / 3 / 10 secs.
4.   Add remaining ingredients (except for bran flakes) in the order listed.
5.   Blitz sp 7 / 10 seconds, to combine. Scrape.

6.   Knead for 5 minutes.
7.   Tip onto a Thermomat or greased bowl, cover and leave to rest for 20 minutes.
8.   Punch down dough and pat/roll out to a 30cm x 25cm rectangle.
9.   Roll tightly into a log shape to fit your greased bread tin.
10.   Slash surface if desired.
11.   Spray lightly with water and sprinkle with bran flakes (optional).
12.   Prove for 30-40 minutes, until doubled.
13.   Place into a cold oven set to 180C, and bake for 30 minutes or until cooked when tested.
14.   Cool immediately on a rack.

BROWN RICE BREAD

A fantastic way to use up leftover cooked rice, you could use brown rice for an even healthier option.

Makes one loaf

Preparation time:
Preparation: 1h 30mins
Baking: 30mins

Accessories you'll need:
TM31/TM5
Spatula

Ingredients:
325 grams water, warm
2 teaspoons Yeast
 pinch sugar
350 grams bakers flour
130 grams wholemeal flour
2 teaspoons bread improver
1 tablespoon Gluten flour
1 level teaspoon salt
130 grams cooked rice (or 65 grams raw rice: basmati, brown, long grain)
1 heaped teaspoon poppy seeds, plus extra for sprinkling

Method:
1.   Place all ingredients into bowl, except for rice and poppy seeds.
2.   Slowly move speed dial to 7, and mix until combined. About 15 seconds. Scrape.
3.   Add rice and poppy seeds.
4.   Knead knead, 5 minutes.
5.   Tip onto a silicone mat or greased bowl and cover lightly. Leave to

rest for 15 minutes.

6.   Punch down dough and pat out to a rectangle. Roll to fit your loaf size tin.

7.   Cover lightly with greased cling wrap and leave to double in size or until crowned the top of the tin by 2cm.

8.   Spray lightly with water and sprinkle with extra poppy seeds (optional).

9.   Place in a cold oven set to 190C for 30 minutes or until cooked when tested.

10.   Cool on a wire rack.

GERMAN VOLLKORNBROT

A hearty wholegrain bread that is a staple in European homes. Delicious as an open sandwich with your favourite toppings or toasted with jam and butter!

Makes one loaf

Preparation time:
Preparation: 2hours
Baking: 40mins

Accessories you'll need:
TM31/TM5
Spatula
Measuring Cup

Ingredients:
Soaked Grains

25 grams pepitas

25 grams pearl barley

25 grams millet

50 grams sunflower seeds

20 grams flax seeds

20 grams rolled oats

15 grams polenta

15 grams sesame seeds

20 grams chia seeds

250 grams hot water

Dough
1 quantity soaked grains, from above
1.5 teaspoons salt
400 grams bakers flour (may possibly need more)
10 grams honey
2 teaspoons Dutch cocoa

2 teaspoons dried yeast
2 teaspoons bread improver
10 grams olive oil
160 grams water (add 120g to start and more if necessary)

Soaking the grains:

Place grains in a bowl and add hot water. Stir to combine and leave to soak overnight.

To make the dough:

1.   Place pre-soaked grains and remaining ingredients in the bowl in the order listed, noting to add only 160g water and more if necessary, once you commence kneading.
2.   Blitz sp 7 / 20 seconds using spatula to assist if necessary. Scrape.
3.   Knead 5 minutes. Check consistency, it's ok if the mixture is a bit sticky but if it's too sticky to hold a shape gradually add a little more flour during kneading.
4.   Tip mixture onto a Thermomat or a greased bowl, cover and rest 30 minutes.
5.   Pat out into a rectangle shape, punching out air bubbles.
6.   Shape into a loaf and place into a greased loaf pan. Or place into a greased floured banneton.
7.   Slash if desired and leave to rise in the usual way until mixture crowns above the tin by 2.5cm, about 1 hour.
8.   Lightly spray with water and sprinkle with extra oat flakes if desired.
9.   Place in a cold oven set to 180C. Or a preheated oven with a skillet heating inside, set to 250 (if using a banneton)
10.   Bake for 30-40 minutes or until done when tested and registers at 90+C on a digital thermometer.

WHOLEMEAL CHIA BREAD

The goodness of Chia seeds and wholegrain flour in one delicious loaf...

Makes one loaf (approximately 10 slices)

Preparation time:
Preparation: 1h
Baking: 30mins

Accessories you'll need:
TM31/TM5
Spatula

Ingredients:
300 grams water or whey
1 teaspoon sugar
2 teaspoons yeast (or 30g fresh yeast)
300 grams bakers flour
300 grams wholemeal flour
2 teaspoons Gluten flour
2 teaspoons bread improver
2 teaspoons salt
20 grams olive oil
2 tablespoons chia seeds stirred into 4 tablespoons warm water

Method:
1.   Place water, sugar and yeast into bowl and whizz 15 secs/sp 3
2.   Add remaining ingredients and blend together briefly on sp 7/ 15 secs.
3.   Knead for 6 minutes.
4.   Tip onto a Thermomat and rest 15 minutes.
5.   Punch down dough and mould into a desired shape, either free-form or to fit a loaf tin.
6.   Prove for 30-40 minutes until dough has doubled in size or about

1cm above top of the tin.

7.   Place in a cold oven set to 180c and bake 30 minutes or until cooked.

8.   Cool on a rack.

GF
GLUTEN
FREE

GLUTEN FREE Chia and Mixed Seed bread

A truly delicious and healthy gluten free bread, as sensational toasted as it is fresh. A must-have gluten free basic for every home cook!

Makes 1 loaf (10 slices)

Preparation time:
Preparation: 1h
Baking: 30mins

Accessories you'll need:
TM31/TM5
Spatula

Ingredients:
2 tablespoons chia seeds, soaked in 6 tablespoons of water
200 grams brown rice
1 teaspoon salt
300 grams GF Flour (plain or self-raising gluten-free flour)
3 teaspoons GF baking powder (omit if using SR flour)
2 tablespoons sugar
1 heaped tablespoon Xanthan gum
20 grams dried yeast
2 eggs
30 grams olive oil
400 grams water
30 grams pepitas, plus a little extra for sprinkling
25 grams sunflower seeds, plus a little extra for sprinkling

Method:
1.   Soak chia in water in a small cup (see ingredients). Set aside.
2.   Place rice into bowl and mill sp 9 / 1.5 mins. Scrape and leave in bowl.
3.   Add remaining ingredients in the order listed, adding the pre-

soaked chia seeds last.

4.   Combine sp4.5 / 30 secs until combined, using your spatula to assist.

5.   Spray a loaf tin with non-stick cooking spray.

6.   Spread mixture into tin...smooth the top.

7.   Prove covered for 30-40 minutes or until doubled in size.

8.   Spray lightly with water and sprinkle with seeds if desired.

9.   Bake in a preheated 190C oven for 30-40 minutes or until cooked.

10.   Cool on a wire rack

Thermify Me Top Tips:

*   Shape as a loaf or rolls depending on what you prefer.

GLUTEN FREE Cheese and Onion bread

A delicious bread served fresh or toasted with scrumptious lashings of butter which can be made either gluten free or with regular flour.

Makes 8 portions

Preparation time: 55 minutes
Preparation: 20 minutes
Baking: 35 minutes

Accessories you'll need:
TM31/TM5
Spatula

Ingredients:
Onions
1 onion, peeled and quartered
1 tablespoon olive oil

Dough
200 grams milk
40 grams Butter, chopped
2 eggs
300 grams GF plain flour
1 tablespoon GF baking powder
1 teaspoon caster sugar
1 teaspoon salt
115 grams Grated Cheddar Cheese
1 tablespoon dried onion or chive flakes, optional

Method:
Cook the onions.

Preheat oven to 190C, grease and line a loaf tin.

1. Place onion into bowl and chop sp 4.5/10 secs.
2. Add oil and cook Varoma/3 mins/sp1. Leave in bowl.
3. Add butter, milk and eggs. Mix sp3/ 5 secs.
4. Add remaining ingredients in order (except for optional dried onions/chives).
5. Mix sp 4.5/20-30 secs using reverse speed setting. You may need to use your spatula to assist.
6. Spread into loaf tin, spray lightly with water and sprinkle with optional dried onions/chives and bake for 30-40 minutes or until cooked when tested.
7. Leave in tin for 10 minutes before turning onto a wire rack to cool.

GLUTEN FREE Honey, Almond, and Cinnamon squares

A delightfully crunchy slice which can be made gluten free or with regular flour. Perfect for lunchboxes, afternoon tea, or a decadent guilt-free snack!

Makes 12 portions

Preparation time: 50 minutes
Preparation: 20 minutes
Baking: 30mins

Accessories you'll need:
TM31/TM5
Spatula

Ingredients:
Dough
65 grams Butter
50 grams brown sugar
60 grams ground almonds
110 grams Gluten free or regular plain flour

Honey, Almond and Cinnamon topping
80 grams Butter
50 grams honey
100 grams flaked almonds
cinnamon sugar, for dusting

Method:
Dough
Preheat oven to 190C and grease and line a 20 x 30 cm slice tin.

1.   Place butter, brown sugar and almond meal into bowl.
2.   Melt at 70c / 2 mins/ sp 2. Scrape

3.   Add vanilla and flour.
4.   Blend sp 4 / 20 seconds. Add a dash of milk or water if it's a little dry.
5.   Spread into prepared slice tin and bake for 15 minutes until golden brown.
6.   Remove from oven when done but leave in the tray.

Honey, Almond and Cinnamon topping
1.   Weigh the butter and honey into the bowl.
2.   Set temperature to 100C / 3 minutes / sp.2. It needs to simmer for a few minutes to turn into a golden colour.
3.   Add the flaked almonds and combine using the reverse speed setting/ sp 1 / 10 seconds.
4.   Spread mixture evenly on the prepared base, and bake again for 15 minutes until the top is golden and bubbling. Sprinkle with a little cinnamon sugar.
5.   Cut into squares when cold to serve.

SWEET ❤ BREADS

YEASTED CINNAMON BREAD

A delicious cross between a bread and a cake...try it warm or toasted and slathered in cinnamon butter!

Makes one loaf

Preparation time:
Preparation: 1h 30mins
Baking: 30mins

Accessories you'll need:
TM31/TM5
Spatula

Ingredients:
Dough
230 grams milk
120 grams Butter
2 teaspoons dry yeast
60 grams sugar
3 eggs, room temperature
600 grams bakers flour
2 teaspoons bread improver
1 teaspoon salt

Cinnamon butter spread
60 grams sugar
2 tablespoons cinnamon
40 grams Butter

To make the dough:
1.   Melt butter and milk in bowl, 37C/ 5 mins/ sp 3
2.   Add yeast and blend sp 2/ 10 secs
3.   Add sugar and eggs, sp 3 / 20 secs.

4.   Add flour, bread improver and salt.

5.   Blitz by bringing dial slowly to sp 7/ 15 secs. If mixture is to sticky add an extra tablespoon of flour.

6.   Knead for 5 mins.

7.   Tip contents onto a silicone mat or greased bowl and leave (covered) to rest for 15 mins. Meanwhile, prepare the cinnamon butter spread.

To make the cinnamon butter spread:

1.   Combine sugar and cinnamon in a small bowl.

2.   Melt butter in a small bowl in the microwave.

Assembly:

1.   Pat dough out into a rectangle measuring 40cm long x width of your bread tin.

2.   Brush liberally with butter.

3.   Sprinkle with cinnamon sugar.

4.   Roll up tightly into a roll shape, taking care to match width to your bread pan. Pinch ends together.

5.   Place seam side down into a greased bread pan. Cover lightly with cling wrap and leave to prove in a warm place until dough has crowned above the tin by about 2cm.

To make the glaze:

1.   Lightly whisk the egg and milk in a small bowl and gently glaze the surface of the bread.

2.   Place into a cold oven set to 150 fan and bake for 30-35 minutes or until cooked when tested.

3.   Cool on a rack.

RASPBERRY BRIOCHE

Oh so delicious filled with your favourite jam or spread... best eaten on the day it's baked or frozen if you want some for later!

Makes one loaf (approximately 14 portions)

Preparation time:
Preparation: 1h 30mins
Baking: 25mins

Accessories you'll need:
TM31/TM5
Spatula

Ingredients:
2 teaspoons dried yeast
45 grams water
150 grams milk
40 grams sugar
460 grams bakers flour
2 teaspoons bread improver (optional, but makes a difference)
80 grams Butter, softened and chopped
2 eggs
1 teaspoon salt
1/3 cup raspberry jam, or any favourite such as Nutella.

Method:
1.   Measure water and milk into the bowl and set to 37C / 3 mins / sp2
2.   Add all ingredients in the order listed, except for the raspberry jam.
3.   Blend briefly on sp 7/ 20 seconds. Scrape.
4.   Knead for 5 minutes.
5.   Rest on a Thermomat or in a greased covered bowl for 20 minutes.
6.   Punch dough down and shape into a rectangle 25 x 35cm.
7.   Roll from the long edge into a tight cylinder.

8. Cut into 7-8 lumps.
9. Shape by rolling into circles and add a heaped teaspoon of jam into the centre of each circle.
10. Gather up edges and pinch closed.
11. Grease a 20-23cm springform tin and place rolls inside, seam side down.
12. Cover and leave to rise 30-40 minutes, until double in size.
13. Gently brush with milk and sprinkle with cinnamon sugar.
14. Place in a cold oven set to 160C for 25 minutes.
15. Serve while still warm..

CHOC-WALNUT BABA

Simply delicious fresh or toasted and spread with lashings of butter!

Makes one loaf

Preparation time:

Preparation: 2h
Baking: 35mins

Accessories you'll need:

TM31/TM5
Spatula

Ingredients:

Dough

100 grams milk
115 grams unsalted butter, chopped
2.5 teaspoons yeast dry
80 grams caster sugar
550 grams bakers flour
2 teaspoons bread improver
3 eggs
50 grams water
Dash vanilla extract
1 teaspoon salt

Filling

175 grams walnuts
40 grams Butter, melted
40 grams caster sugar
1 teaspoon cinnamon
5 heaped tablespoons Nutella, to taste
90 grams choc bits, or to taste

To make the dough:
1.   Melt butter and milk in bowl, 37C/ 5 mins/ sp 3
2.   Add remaining ingredients in the order listed.
3.   Blitz by bringing dial slowly to sp 7/ 15 secs. If mixture is to sticky add an extra tablespoon of flour.
4.   Knead for 5 mins.
5.   Tip contents onto a Thermomat or greased bowl and leave (covered) to rest for 15 mins. Meanwhile, prepare the choc walnut filling

To make the filling:
1.   Combine sugar and cinnamon in a small bowl. Set aside.
2.   Melt butter in a small bowl in the microwave. Set aside
3.   Place walnuts into the bowl.
4.   Chop briefly sp 4, 3-5 secs. Set all aside.

Assembly:
1.   Pat dough out into a rectangle measuring 30 long x 25cm wide
2.   Spread liberally with Nutella
3.   Sprinkle with cinnamon sugar.
4.   Sprinkle with walnuts and choc bits, and drizzle with the melted butter. Roll up tightly into a roll shape. Pinch ends together.
5.   Slice through dough to make app 8-10 pieces. Stack on top of each other in a well greased baba tin. Or place the rolled tube into the prepared tin.
6.   Cover lightly with cling wrap and leave to prove in a warm place until dough has crowned near the top of the tin or slightlyabove.
7.   Bake in a cold oven set to 180C and bake for 30-35 minutes or until cooked when tested. If it starts to darken too quickly, reduce the temp to 170C.
8.   Leave in tin for 5 minutes before carefully tipping onto a wire rack to cool.

BUN-ANA EASTER LOAF

What do you get when you cross a Hot Cross Bun with delicious moist banana bread? Bun-ana Easter Loaf!

Makes 1 loaf or 8 buns

Preparation time:
Preparation: 2h
Baking: 30mins

Accessories you'll need:
TM31/TM5
Spatula

Ingredients:
55 grams caster sugar

2 teaspoons dried yeast

50 grams warm water

2 large ripe bananas, (should be approximately 280g when peeled)

1 egg

525 grams bakers flour

1.5 teaspoons mixed spice

1/2 teaspoon cinnamon

50 grams Butter

To make the dough:
1.   Weigh sugar, water. yeast, chopped banana and egg into the bowl.
2.   Blend briefly sp 4/5 seconds
3.   Add flour, spices and butter to bowl.
4.   Blend briefly sp 7/20 seconds.
5.   Knead for 5 minutes.
6.   Tip mixture onto a Thermomat, or lightly floured surface.
7.   Sprinkle mixed fruit and peel over the top and knead in by hand

until it's all combined.

8.   Shape into a ball and leave to rise (covered) until doubled, sometimes up to an hour.

9.   Punch down dough and shape into 6-8 balls, depending on the size of your pan.

10.   Place them alongside each other in the greased pan...doesn't matter if they are a bit squashed in..

11.   Leave to rise again on a pre-heated **Breadwinner proving mat** (contact us for information), or prove in your usual way, until doubled, up to 50 minutes.

To make the paste:

1.   In a small bowl blend paste ingredients to a smooth paste.

2.   Fill a small piping bag with the mixture and pipe crosses over the proven rolls.

3.   Pop into your pre-heated oven and bake for around 30 minutes, or until cooked.

To make the glaze:

1.   Combine glaze ingredients in a microwave safe bowl, and heat in microwave until the sugar has dissolved.

2.   Brush glaze liberally over the hot loaf once removed from the oven.

Thermify Me Top Tips:

* Make it without the crosses as a regular fruit loaf.

* If you don't like mixed peel, omit it and add extra dried fruit.

If you've enjoyed the Monica Hailes Cooking School's *Bread for the Thermomix* you'll love our Facebook page! Come and join us:

Facebook
Thermify Me
Thermify Me Breadwinners

To keep up-to-date with all things Thermomix, cooking, baking and for early-bird pre-order on all our upcoming Cooking School cookbooks, join our Thermify Me newsletter.

COMING SOON

Monica Hailes Cooking School's *Cakes and Biscuits for the Thermomix*

Monica Hailes Cooking School's *German Favourites for the Thermomix*

Monica Hailes Cooking School's *Soups and Savoury Treats for the Thermomix*

CPSIA information can be obtained
at www.ICGtesting.com
Printed in the USA
LVHW070206260119
605390LV00005B/59/P